Deserts

By Jan Anderson

Contents

Introduction

There are deserts in many parts
of the world.
Deserts are very dry places
because there is so little rain.

Most deserts have very hot weather
during the day.
At night, they can be freezing cold.

Many deserts are almost bare
because there is not enough rain
for plants to grow.

It is hard for people and animals
to live in deserts.
People have different kinds of homes
to keep out the heat.
Some animals live under the ground
during the day so they stay cool.

How Deserts Form

A desert is a place with very little water and only a few plants.
If there is no rain, or too much wind, a desert starts to form.

Sometimes, people turn land into deserts
when they cut down too many trees.
There are no plants left
to keep the soil together.

Wind storms blow away the soil
and the land becomes bare.

Types of Deserts

Most deserts are rocky.

Some deserts are made up
of very big rocks.
Other deserts are filled
with lots of little stones.

A few deserts are made of sand.
The most famous sandy desert
is called the Sahara Desert.
It is in Africa.
Hills of sand
have been piled up by the wind.

Water in the Desert

Some water in the desert
comes from a small amount of rain,
or from dew.

In some deserts,
it has not rained for years.

DID YOU KNOW?

Some areas in a desert
start to crack
when it has not rained
for a long time.

Sometimes, there is water
deep under the desert.
People dig wells to get to this water.

People in the Desert

People have always lived in deserts.
The days are hot and the nights are cold.
During the day, there is almost nowhere
to get out of the wind and sun.

Many desert people are nomads.
They move from one place to another
to find food and water.
Sometimes they find water at an oasis.

DID YOU KNOW?

An oasis is like a pond in the desert.
The water at an oasis
comes from under the ground.

Homes

In some deserts, there are oases
where there is enough water
for people to live.

The people build houses nearby.
The houses have thick walls
and small windows.
In the daytime, these houses stay cool
when it is hot outside.
At night, the houses are warm
when it is cold outside.

In some deserts,
people live under the ground.
They dig rooms out of the rock.
The houses are cool,
and they are safe from sandstorms.

Nomads who live in the desert
have tents made of goats' skins.
When they move around,
they take their tents with them.

Finding Food

In some deserts,
people keep goats for meat and milk.
Goats can eat many different plants.

People also get milk from camels.

Many years ago, Aborigines in Australia
spent most of the day
finding food in the desert.

They hunted kangaroos for meat.
They also ate grubs
that they found among the roots
of desert plants.

17

Desert plants

Plants in the desert have to live
with very little rain.
Some plants have long roots
that find water under the ground.
Others have leaves
that soak up dew at night.

Many plants have seeds
that only sprout after it has rained.

Some plants have leaves like needles.
Because of their shape,
these leaves do not lose as much water
as flat leaves do.

The cactus is a plant
that lives in the desert.
It holds water in its stems.

Desert Animals

Many desert animals live under the ground, away from the sun.
Some of them come out at night to feed, when it is cool.

Many different insects live in the desert.
There are flies, wasps, and beetles.
There are lizards, too.
They eat insects,
and hardly ever
need to drink water.

In some deserts,
there are scorpions
that dig burrows
and only come out at night.

Desert animals must look hard
to find water.

Some animals lick the dew on leaves.
Other animals, like camels and kangaroos,
get water from the leaves that they eat.

DID YOU KNOW?

Snakes hide in cracks
and holes in rocks,
to get out of the heat.

Camels

Dear Mustafa,

Last week, Father and I walked across the desert
to a market town, with the camel train.

We walked for many days in the hot sun.
When we reached an oasis,
the camels drank and drank.

All the camels carried heavy loads.
It is just as well camels have wide feet
or they would have sunk
into the soft sand.

We are now at the market town.
In two days, we will set off for home.

Your friend, Ahmed

DID YOU KNOW?

Camels can drink 26 gallons of water at one time.

It is very hard to live in deserts. But people, plants, and animals have learned how to survive.

Questions

1. When do some deserts start to crack?
2. What is an oasis?
3. What kind of tree often grows at oases?
4. Where do snakes hide
   to get away from the heat?
5. How much water can camels drink at one time?

Glossary

bare	empty or with no covering
dew	drops of water that cover the ground and plants during the night
nomad	a person who does not live in one place
oasis	place in the desert with water and trees
sprout	start to grow
wells	deep holes in the ground filled with water